DUNG BEETLES
NAVIGATE BY STARLIGHT

SARAH WATKINSON

INDEPENDENT INNOVATIVE INTERNATIONAL

Published by Cinnamon Press
Meirion House,
Glan yr afon,
Tanygrisiau
Blaenau Ffestiniog,
Gwynedd, LL41 3SU
www.cinnamonpress.com

The right of Sarah Watkinson to be identified as author of this work has been asserted by her in accordance with the Copyright, Designs and Patent Act, 1988. Copyright © 2015 Sarah Watkinson.
ISBN: 978-1-910836-58-3

British Library Cataloguing in Publication Data. A CIP record for this book can be obtained from the British Library.

Designed and typeset in Palatino by Cinnamon Press.

Cover design by Jan Fortune.

Printed in Poland

Cinnamon Press is represented in the UK by Inpress Ltd and in Wales by the Welsh Books Council

Acknowledgements

I would like to thank Jenny Lewis of The Poet's House, Oxford, for her encouragement, constructive criticism and guidance; Jo Bell's 52 Group for inspiration and generous critique through 2014 and beyond; and Anthony Watkinson, who knows what my poems are about.

I owe special thanks to Nicholas Bielby, who published my first poems in *Pennine Platform*, and also to Jane Draycott, Carrie Etter, Philip Gross, David Morley and Penelope Shuttle, whose tuition enabled me to write or revise several of the poems in this pamphlet.

Poems in this collection appeared in the following publications: 'The Enemy Within' appeared in *Pennine Platform 77*, 2015; 'Aspergillus' appeared in *Litmus*, Autumn 2016; 'Dung Beetles Navigate by Starlight' was highly commended in the Norwich Writers' Circle Open Poetry Competition, 2013; 'Summer's Lease' was commended in the RSPB Rialto poetry competition 2014; part of 'Borderland' appeared in the StAnza Poetry Map of Scotland (online); 'Siberian Tiger' appeared in *Nutshells and Nuggets,* July 2014 (online); 'A Room and a Half' appeared in *The Rialto* 82, Winter 2015; 'Getting the Bones Right' won joint first prize for sonnets in the Ware Poets' Open Poetry Competition 2015; 'Pelagic' appeared in *Antiphon*, January 2016 (online); 'Ash' appeared in *Pennine Platform 77*, 2015; 'A Paradigm Shift in Ornithology' won second prize in the Battered Moons Poetry Competition 2014.

'The Wood-Wide Web' is inspired by 'Mould Music, Philip Gross from *Love Songs of Carbon*, Bloodaxe Books, 2015.

The title poem, 'Dung Beetles Navigate by Starlight' was prompted by Dacke, M., Baird, E., Byrne, M., Scholtz, Clarke H., and Warrant, Eric J. (2013), 'Dung Beetles Use the Milky Way for Orientation', *Current Biology*.

Contents

Dung Beetles Navigate by Starlight

The Wood-Wide Web

For Philip Gross, antiphon to 'Mould Music'

Underfoot, sharers
in the earth,
with one tree
or another,

they grow nets
to catch salvage:

scatterings of wood,
washings of foliage...

store and return salts, for a fee
paid in summer sap.

They whisper their way
into roots, and become

chimaera: *Mycorrhiza*,
rufous, violaceous, melanised,
down in the dark.

Stinkhorns, earthstars,
deceivers, chanterelles –

their spore-launchers – come up
in their own time, in warm damp.

They deal us whatever helps them:
disgust, death, delicatessen, musk.

Honey Fungus

Parts of me are excited, they sense a tree
felled by snow, stressed till the fibres rip
and the whole rich mass thumps down.

I stir in the earth. My hundred probes
taste air in the caves and sumps of soil.
They rise to dampness, and emerge

into a bark-roofed underpass. There
my body squeezes close, flat to the bast,
and signals me. I shift shape and flow,

burning and melting wood, and as I go
I feel sweet monomers tingle on my skin
infusing me with power. I press on.

Reading the Genes

For Igor Grigoriev

How timber disintegrates, strangely soft
under fingering mycelium.
The sub-floor won't bear,
charred and dark
like burnt trees.

In the microscope
threads creep and meet,
in a random net.

The chemistry is strange –
what's left of wood
an Angstrøm bombsite
of nonsense molecules, a litter
of chair-springs and clock-springs.

At JGI, Stonehenge of the DNA,
priests at last descry
the nuclear instructions
for multiple, powerful, micro-explosions.

Chance Governs All

Imagine you're a spore,
a speck of life powder
fuelled for flight, DNA
and RNA in separate bags.

Feel your skin tight-caged
in orange, ultraviolet-proof
for that black sunlit upper air;
chitin-reinforced, steel-strong.

Vortexed up from the earth,
you sweep the troposphere,
then, downed in driving rain
you're slammed to a stop

at random. Your life depends
on kit in your genes; leaf maps,
germ tubes, a blowtorch for wood
and every enzyme in the book.

The Enemy Within

'The parasite changes the insect's behaviour so that its dead body sends out infecting spores'

An exoskeleton of armoured plates,
eyes for a single photon in the dark,
antennae for a scent a mile away,
wall-walker weaponed with a poison dart—
add knightly virtues, and this insectoid
is Sci-Fi superman *par excellence*

      until the knowing enemy arrives,
and feeds misinformation to his brain,
diverts chivalric instinct, mating, flight,
to a mad urge to climb and cling and stay.
      At last, flesh gone, only a husk remains,
fixed to the tallest stems through wind and rain
his mouldy armour broadcasting the plague,
the independent self dissolved away.

Aspergillus

I hope I'm not seeing my own lung
and that my wheeze and cough like bursting geothermal crust
is a cold, and not these silvered fungal fingers
driving dark tunnels through bronchial epithelium.
I raise my eyes from the scientific paper
and let my focus slide to the end of the garden
where the dogs' graves are, under the Sturmer Pippin.

Dung Beetles Navigate by Starlight

I track my treasure home on star beams, hide
my finds in caverns, steer them clean away,
before I'm stranded in the clueless day
with all my musky gleanings dull and dried.
Straightness is all. The constellations guide
my angled legs. The facets of each eye
lock on to glimmers, sensed how? Who can say?
The system works for me. I'm satisfied.

I know those lines of light shine down for me,
the dung deposited on dewy ground,
a providence. Through moonless dark I see
in multiple dimensions, beacons round,
and every blessed night miraculously
precipitates new turds for me to find.

British Mosses and Liverworts

i.m E.V.Watson

Take a magnifying glass to moss:

so many, and small enough
to be named only in Latin –

worth learning, when it's wet
and the tops are out of sight.

The cells look Escher-tiled
and only just unseen,

a dew-green skin
of water and light

rootless on rock. Between
torrents and summer drought,

moss makes the most of clouds,
spreads photovoltaics to the misted sun.

Some rainy afternoon, walk out. Look down. Enjoy
the treasure hunt: garnet on flooded slabs is *Bryum rubrum*,

bright *Philonotis* aprons a spring, and *Rhacomitrium*
on wind-skimmed summits, dries hoary-grey in summer, like shed wool.

Water-talk: A Phytolinguistic Map
of a Site in the Clun Valley, September 2015

A Stream Bed

The abundant ferns were dumb,
waiting for rain. We knew of,
but could not record,
their well-known liquid accents:
splashes, seepages and drips.

Tree Trunks

Mosses clung to their few words of water,
a tiny fraction of their thesaurus.
We recorded some brittle mutters
from *Tortula ruralis*
(The use of moss killer
accounted for the sundial's silence).

The Kitchen Garden

An imported group of twelve *Lycopersicon* individuals
spoke an idiolect of water butts and taps, a vocabulary
from which *might* and *could be* were missing,
likewise *drought* and *shrivelling*.

The Mill Pond

A large duckweed population, all closely related,
spoke simultaneously in high-pitched anaerobic,
producing a soft sibilance across the surface.

The Banks of the River Clun

Alders lined up to discuss their unique argot, its long-forgotten roots
submerged by currents from the west. Balsam, an exotic, spoke a
Sanskrit patois with frequent plosives. In calm intervals we detected
the liverworts' exhalations.

Summer's Lease

Leaves are a billion islands, countries for the extremely small, who stand on the green shore and survey the endless air with feelers. The land grows under their feet and each one plants its flag further and further out.

Zoom in and walk with us over pillowed cobbles surfaced in bendy glass. Squeeze down through one of our variable-aperture manholes and let us demonstrate the infrastructure. Watch, see how these green palisades are more than mere pit props.

We marvelled at the pulsating solar array and its moist luminosity. The silence was alive and everything was automated. We experienced the light failure response. It felt eerie when the ovoid chloroplasts tipped and rose in unison and the space underneath darkened.

That was in the glory days. You used to have the place to yourself. Then you met another, another, and another, and the crunching became unbearable. Some of them do parthenogenesis. There will be a fall soon.

The First Green Human:
The Observer Interviews Clorinda

with apologies to Elizabeth Day

Her movements are quick. I had expected a plant-like woman to be languorous, but she tells me the morning sunshine has charged her up. *I am particular about wavelength,* she says, *I am useless after midday.*

How do you dress for photosynthesis? I ask. Her lovely face is not obviously green. I wonder where she takes in the light which is her nourishment. She turns to show me. Below the halter neck of cinnamon silk her back is not tanned as I had expected, but the emerald of a chameleon on banana leaves. *I am a one woman power-pack,* she explains, with a disarming grin. *Think of my back as a solar panel. One day everybody will be like me. It's far more efficient to convert people than to cover agricultural land in glass, or have wind turbines looming on every hill.*

So do you eat at all? I ask, spotting an empty bowl and spoon on the rattan table at her elbow. *Bone meal and sea-salt, and the tiniest shots of rare minerals – manganese, zinc and cobalt, when I'm feeling decadent,* she admits.

She sees me noticing her diamond ring, and smiles. *He's non-green,* she confides. *And my green is not passed on. Any kids will have to work for a living.*

On leaving I turn at the gate to wave, but she is already prone again, stretched out viridian on the lawn.

Marine Deposit

Neptune on the Pennine Way,
like a land-lubber cruising,
feels out of his element.

It is all so effortful·
the wind no help to progress
in spite of a gale blowing −

until, against a limestone
outcrop, propped, he sits resting,
and hears the high-pitched voices:

>   *'Sir, you've been away too long'*

>   − crinoids from a sea-bed
>   fossilised in the strata −

and knows his sea-home has been
everywhere once, though shifting;
feels soothed, and bivouacs there.

Borderland

Windy Gyle

Between the clouds and their shadows passing
　　disembodied across bleached moor grass and its bracken patches,
　　I'm on a border strung along a ridge
　　in cloudberries, on black peat. At my back the working Tyne,
　　ahead the salmon roads
　　　　Tweed, Teviot and drowning Till,
　　　　　　beyond, the northward haze,
　　　　　　　　Roman Trimontium, the three hills of Melrose.

Norham Bridge

You can't see a border in the hill-caught water
　　eddying below. From the highest arch
　　it's as though I hear my father's reel, and it's you,
　　pony-tailed, in waders, casting into Scotland
　　laying your line straight above a rise.
　　　　I'm at a crux of water and time:
　　　　　　east, the sea; west the river's source,
　　　　　　　　mist on Eskdalemuir and rain-filled moss.

The Border Union Show at Duns

Here are the sheep: Cheviots and Texels,
　　the year's work incarnate, penned
　　to admire at the edge of the field,
　　away from pipe bands and ponies.
　　But this is no side-show,
　　　　there's weight in the calm voices.
　　　　　　It's like a summit meeting of great farms,
　　　　　　　　the allied kingdoms of this settled border.

Restoring a Farm near Hook Norton

'The plough has had them under hand
And over turned 'em all'

John Clare

We enter by a rain-carved dell, too steep to till,
through an old settlement of flowers in their places.
Thyme and rock-rose colour the sunlight,
bellflower and meadowsweet the shade,

a knot in time. Fields are plain now, only the trim
remains − floral margins on a work-wear livery
of stripes: barley, wheat and rape.
We hanker for Emmonsales Heath
but forget the way back.

Newly unharrowed, the earth
recovers roots slowly. Underground
a motherboard rebuilds, feeding
orchids − fragrant, spotted,
pyramidal − from thin turf.

Everything's come on the wind
or somehow survived. On the hill
we look for the plant community we knew.
Hay rattle clatters at our ankles

but we want our old *millefiori* pasture:
deep-rooted perennials; woven
herbs; hazel, honeysuckle, dogwood −
a tough and speckled tweed.

Organic Chemistry

If I'd had Virgil with me on the school bus
        curving down to the smog-bound river valley,
                he might have shown me the syllabus setters
                    shut inside small rooms

with no light or view, for keeping from children
        what wonders carbon makes: its sheets and spirals,
                libraries of books, the scaffolding of life,
                    our pulsing tissues.

We learned its chemistry through manufactures:
        carbon rings, tight strained, made TNT for bombs,
                with azo nitrogen, new permanent dyes −
                    purposeful studies.

For Professor Alison Smith

In primeval soup
you said, rings
sprang to shape.

Hexagons and pentagons
snapped to spheres,
by chance. Gazebos,

geodesic domes,
nano-cities, self-built
on micro-particles

until this tetrapyrrole
web trapped iron.
An electron catapult,

oxygen-charged,
blood red
to quicken flesh.

Seamus Heaney at the Sheldonian Theatre, Oxford

We left behind
the empty-eyed stone emperors
for an amphitheatre of moss. The god is on stage
like a swan landed on a nymphaeum,
folding his outstretched wings. He reads
of all that he has seen from his wide sky:

> truth mirrored from oceans,
> from mountain-caught pools,
> tubs and wells.

A teacher's question: *'Can this be taught,
should children learn poetry by rote?'*

His Irish voice:
By heart.

Siberian Tiger—

striped black and orange in your dull forest
aren't you a target?   *No.*
My stripes join the ranks of bare trees
and when I stand still
my back is sunset snow.

A Room and a Half (Andrey Khrzhanovsky, 2010)

'Loneliness cubes a man at random'
                          Iosif Brodsky

How do you throw a snowball at yourself?
Or skate a quarter-pipe in a blizzard?
The honey is spun from the comb, the cells are empty.
Can you gather birds with an aviary,
or a bestiary by building a zoo?
Whatever it was, if it is powerful enough it can unhappen.
The ruins are somewhere else, regrowing, biomineralising;
architectural stem cells are rebuilding a conservatoire
and the instruments have got wind of it.

Getting the Bones Right

It takes me more than **one** road kill to pre pare
a mount. If there are **two** I can choose the best
un dam aged bones and **three** is ev en bett er.
Corp ses get smashed if **four** tyres go o ver them.
Rabb its take a bout **five** hours boil ing to clean
the flesh from the bones. **Six** may be nec ess ary.
I re build the ribs, **seven** on each side. See my
hedge hogs. I've mount ed **eight** of those. Rar it ies
like mart ens? Hard er. **Nine** at night in summ er,
ev en as late as **ten,** is best for shy ones.
As a boy, on ly **eleven,** once I dis cov ered
a dead sonn et, just **twelve** lines, the tail miss ing.
I stuck one on, but **thirteen** 'sa symm et ric al.
You need the set of **fourteen** to make it life like.

Pelagic

Rigged for winter gales and the wild northern air
we ride the night swell, lift from the crest foam-light
taking what weather comes; swoop for a sprat
side-slip on up-draughts,   hang on the wind, debonair

until breeding time comes and makes each of us one of a pair
on a rock face reeking with guano, and life's a fight—

    gitawaay Kittiwake gitawaay—with fledglings to flight
        gitawaay to the sea before the turn of the year.

We nest on heights where boulder-lift sweeps our ledge;
washed in our element we take one step, extend
wings that bear us there in the surf's echo—

        sail us up, above the cliff's edge
or down, glissading on streams of wind

      to the dark sea rioting below.

Ash

Grows alone.

Roots grapple rock, mine stone.

Above, a crown of tridents, char-tipped

metal-fretted spears, a phalanx silhouetted

on arctic sky or moon wrack, accepts the rivers of wind,

bends but never breaks. Light-lover of northern upland, away

from tree crowds, forests, southern swathes

of ancient woods, hangers, spinneys

plantations, coverts, chases

earth-moulded

moss-muffled

leaf-gloomed.

Wind-spread

rain-silvered

reared skyward

on the distant hill

Thor's steed. Old Yggdrasil

Holly Bush Roost

Night-green spiny shelter
for clouds of twittering starlings,
it's high as the house and Gherkin-shaped.
They arrive every dusk and fly into its heart
in waves, like trainloads of reverse commuters,
a mirror population that bustles in at evening
from Aldgate Station, filling floor by floor
of deserted offices, every one heading for
a work station, parking overnight bags
in desk drawers. I wonder, as each
bird dashes through the skin
of prickles, into the core,
if it targets a special twig
so the bush fills in layers.
Maybe infra-red imaging
would show their bodies
pale, arranged in rows.

A Paradigm Shift in Ornithology

Birds are made of light.
The chorus is dawn.
Every morning, energy crystallises
on solid objects: twigs, rooftops.

When brilliance breaks on the horizon
birds are generated at every wavelength
from quick bluetits to red cardinals,
or the whole iridescence of a magpie's wing.

Their bodies are different from ours.
Caged, they may clot to solidity, but free
they don't age, you don't see old birds
fly more slowly, perch for longer, grey at the wings, get fat.

If shot, they fool you with implausible remains—
a puff of feathers, a single wing in the bracken. Cats
are disappointed with their trophy: just claws and guts.

If the morning is sunny, when each bird appears
spare energy is transformed to song,
although you can't hum the tune.

At sunset they darken and vanish—
new ones will condense again at first light